NERDING OUT ABOUT

ROLE-PLAYING

NERD
CULTURE

VIRGINIA LOH-HAGAN

45TH PARALLEL PRESS

Published in the United States of America by Cherry Lake Publishing Group
Ann Arbor, Michigan
www.cherrylakepublishing.com

Reading Adviser: Beth Walker Gambro, MS, Ed., Reading Consultant, Yorkville, IL
Book Designer: Joseph Hatch

Photo Credits: © Serhiibobyk, Adobe Stock, cover, title page; © Stasia04/Shutterstock, 4; © Kiselev Andrey Valerevich/Shutterstock, 7; © Piyato/Shutterstock, 8; © David Pimborough/Shutterstock, 10; Unknown author, CC BY-SA 4.0 via Wikimedia Commons, 12; © Andrey Sayfutdinov/Shutterstock, 15; © Oakland Images/Shutterstock, 16; © Master1305/Shutterstock, 19; © Master1305/Shutterstock, 20; © Esther H. Derksen/Shutterstock, 22; © Michaela Pilch/Shutterstock, 24; © FlexDreams/Shutterstock, 26; © SashaMagic/Shutterstock, 28; © Markus Wissmann/Shutterstock, 29

45th Parallel Press is an imprint of Cherry Lake Publishing Group.

Library of Congress Cataloging-in-Publication Data

Names: Loh-Hagan, Virginia, author.
Title: Nerding out about role-playing / Virginia Loh-Hagan.
Description: Ann Arbor, Michigan : 45th Parallel Press, 2024. | Series:
   Nerd culture | Audience: Grades 4-6 | Summary: "Nerding Out About
   Role-Playing covers the wonderfully nerdy world of role-playing: from
   cosplay to DnD. This 45th Parallel hi-lo series includes considerate
   vocabulary and high-interest content"-- Provided by publisher.
Identifiers: LCCN 2023035095 | ISBN 9781668939369 (paperback) | ISBN
   9781668938324 (hardcover) | ISBN 9781668940709 (ebook) | ISBN
   9781668942055 (pdf)
Subjects: LCSH: Fantasy games--Juvenile literature. |
   Role-playing--Juvenile literature.
Classification: LCC GV1469.6 .L65 2024 | DDC 793.93--dc23/eng/20230818
LC record available at https://lccn.loc.gov/2023035095

Cherry Lake Publishing Group would like to acknowledge the work of the Partnership for 21st Century Learning, a Network of Battelle for Kids. Please visit Battelle for Kids online for more information.

Note from publisher: Websites change regularly, and their future contents are outside of our control. Supervise children when conducting any recommended online searches for extended learning opportunities.

Printed in the United States of America

Dr. Virginia Loh-Hagan is an author and educator. She is currently the Director of the Asian Pacific Islander Desi American (APIDA) Center at San Diego State University and the Co-Executive Director of The Asian American Education Project. She lives in San Diego with her very tall husband and very naughty dogs.

TABLE OF CONTENTS

Nerds are now trendy. Many nerds play hero roles in movies today.

LIVING THE NERDY LIFE

It's finally cool to be a nerd. Nerd culture is everywhere. It's in movies. It's on TV. It's in video games. It's in books. Everyone is talking about it. Everyone is watching it. Everyone is doing it. There's no escaping nerd culture.

Nerds and sports fans are alike. They have a lot in common. Instead of sports, nerds like nerdy things. Magic is nerdy. Science fiction is nerdy. Superheroes are nerdy. Nerds obsess over these interests. They're huge fans. They have a great love for a topic. They learn all they can. They spend hours on their hobbies. Hobbies are activities. Nerds hang with others who feel the same.

Nerds form **fandoms**. Fandoms are nerd networks. They're communities of fans. Nerds host online group chats. They host meetings. They host **conventions**. Conventions are large gatherings. They have speakers. They have workshops. They're also called **expos**. Tickets sell fast. Everyone wants to go. Nerd conventions are the place to be.

Nerd culture is on the rise. It's very popular. But it didn't used to be. Nerds used to be bullied. They were made fun of. They weren't seen as cool. They'd rather study than party. This made them seem odd. They were seen as different. Not anymore! Today, nerds rule!

Growing nerd fandoms have led to more role-playing with elaborate costumes.

People have fun acting like their role-play characters.

CHAPTER 1

PLAYING THE PART

Role-playing (RP) is acting. People play a **role**. Roles are characters. People choose a character. They act like that character. They change their looks. They change how they act. They pretend. They can be anything. They can be anyone.

Role-playing is part of nerd culture. It plays a big part. Nerds are fantasy fans. They're science fiction fans. They're comic fans. They admire characters. Some become fan artists. They draw pictures of their favorite characters. Some move into **cosplay**. Cosplayers role-play as their favorite characters. They act like them. They wear costumes. They escape into their own worlds.

Tabletop role-playing games often use dice with different numbers of sides for different actions.

Nerds also role-play when playing games. These games are called **role-playing games** (RPG). These games require players to become characters. They can create their own characters. These are called **original characters** (OCs). Players build OCs as they play. Or players can use **premade characters**. Premade means already created.

Players can do things they normally might not do. They can be creative. This makes games more fun. No one knows what will happen. No one knows how players will react. Anything is possible!

RP communities are key. Fans interact with each other. They do this in character. They build connections. They do this as characters. They also do this as players.

The Celtic festival of Samhain is the origin of modern-day Halloween in the United States. People love role-playing on Halloween!

CHAPTER 2

BEYOND HALLOWEEN

Actors dress up. They pretend to be characters. They perform on stage. They perform in movies. They entertain people. This has been happening since ancient times. Ancient means a long time ago.

What about people who don't act? Many dress up for Halloween. They do this once a year. Halloween is celebrated on October 31. It started more than 2,000 years ago. It started in ancient Scotland. It celebrated the end of summer. It marked the start of winter. Winter was known as dark times. People thought ghosts came out. People dressed in scary costumes. They wanted to hide from the ghosts. Halloween spread to the United States. People dressed up for fun.

TV became popular in the 1950s. This brought a craze for pop culture. People watched superheroes on TV. They read comic books. Soon, they wanted to be those characters.

Role-playing in games has been around for a while. Cultures have acted out their histories. People have played games in different roles. An example is murder mystery games. People host dinner parties. They solve crimes. **War games** are played. Players pretend to fight each other. An early example is chess.

In the 1970s, RPGs emerged. They were different from ball games. They were different from card games. They were different from family board games. They require players to be characters. They have strategy. They can keep being played. They don't have winners or losers. They just have players.

Halloween costumes used to be scary. Today, they reflect pop culture.

Cosplay started in Japan. It became popular in the 1990s.

CHAPTER 3

PLAYING PRETEND

Nerd culture has different RP examples. Cosplay is the most popular. It means costume play. It's a performance art. Cosplayers dress as their favorite characters. They're inspired by many sources. They go to fan conventions. They go to parties. They go to parades. They show off their costumes.

Cosplay can be simple. It can be fancy. Cosplayers wear costumes. They have props. They wear makeup.

There are cosplay contests. Cosplayers must make their own costumes. They perform an act. They pose. They're interviewed. Winners best reflect their characters' personalities.

Cosplayers model for pictures. Some post pictures online. Some sell their images.

NERD LINGO!

BARKS

Barks are phrases. They're used in combat role-plays. They're shouted. An example is yelling, "Bomb!"

BUFFING

Buffing uses magic. It makes skills better. It increases powers.

CANTRIPS

Cantrips are small magic spells. They're used by magician characters.

DPS

DPS means damage per second. It refers to characters who cause damage.

GLAMOUR

A glamour is a magical spell. It's used to disguise characters.

HUMANS

Humans are a species in role-playing games. The word is capitalized.

JOBBERS

Jobbers are fighters. They always lose.

LORE

Lore means content. Extra content can be added. It shouldn't clash with the story. It must fit the role-playing setting.

META-PLOT

Role-playing games have stories. Each story has its own plot. Meta-plot is the bigger story.

TANKS

Tanks are characters. They fight enemies. They take hits. They buy time for the heroes.

TPK

TPK means total party kill. This is when all characters die.

Reenactments are role-playing events. People act out a past time period. People dress in clothes from that time. They do activities from that time. They eat foods from that time. They talk like people did back then.

Museums host reenactments. These help people learn about history. **Buffs** also host these events. Buffs are fans. Civil War buffs are an example. They love learning about the American Civil War (1861–1865). They act out battles.

The **English Renaissance** is a time period. It took place from the 1400s to the 1600s. It's the setting for some fantasy stories. Fairs about this period are held. They're very popular.

People love wearing period costumes. Period means historical times.

There are two main types of RPG. One type is CRPG. It stands for computer role-playing games. They include video games. The other type is TTRPG. TTRPG means tabletop role-playing games. They include board games. They're played around a table.

Both are special games. Players create characters. They play as their characters. Their characters have names. They have background stories. They're called **player characters**. A series of games is called a **campaign**. They can last for months. Some last years.

These games have fictional settings. They have rules. Players choose their actions. They talk about their moves. They discuss them with other players. They create the game outcomes together.

World of Warcraft is a well-known CRPG.

NERD TO KNOW!

Yaya Han is a Chinese American. She was born in 1980. She designs costumes. She's a cosplayer. She's a professional. She turned cosplaying into a job. She judges at cosplay contests. Her designs win awards. Han is invited to conventions. She's one of the first expo stars. She's been on TV shows. She became famous. She created her own brand. She sells her own cosplay materials. She's written a book. She first started cosplaying in 1999. She went to a convention. The convention was the Anime Expo. Han was hooked. She loved cosplay. She taught herself to sew. She bought a used sewing machine. She bought a used sewing book. She made her own costumes. She's made more than 400 costumes. She helped make cosplay an art form. Before being a cosplayer, she was a fan artist. She drew images of characters. Cosplay gave her a new life. She said, "I don't have to draw my favorite characters. I can become my favorite characters."

Dungeons & Dragons has different editions. These each have different sets of rules.

Dungeons & Dragons (D&D) was created in 1974. It was inspired by fantasy stories. It was also inspired by war games. It made RPG popular.

Players play in character the whole time. They form a party. They go on **quests**. Quests are adventures. They're journeys. Players solve problems. They fight in battles. They fight monsters. They get treasures. They have powers. They earn points. They try to rise in levels. The higher the level, the better.

Game masters (GM) are in charge. They decide the setting. They narrate the story. They decide the rules. They use dice. They roll the dice to decide outcomes.

TTRPG led to LARP. LARP means live action role-playing. This is a live game. In TTRPG, players describe their actions. In LARP, players act them out. They dress up. They meet each other. They act like their characters.

Game masters host LARP games. They invite players. They decide the setting. They decide the quests. They decide the rules. LARP games have more freedom than TTRPG. The rules aren't as strict.

There are different LARP themes. They can be fantasy. They can be science fiction. They can be history. LARP games can be small. They can be big.

LARP games are fun because people can pretend to be their characters!

TOO NERDY!

Players know they're role-playing. They know they're
playing parts. They know they're humans. But otherkin
are different. Being otherkin is an identity. Otherkin
ask, "What does it mean to be human?" Otherkin
don't think they're fully human. They feel trapped in
human bodies. They know they look human. They know
they're born human. But they feel they're something
else. Some think they're animals. Some think they're
monsters. Some think they're cartoon characters.
Some think they're plants. Some think they're weather.
Some think they're things. Some think they're aliens.
Many otherkin believe in parallel universes. They
think multiple worlds exist. They think people can live
different lives. The otherkin community started in the
1960s. It grew out of elf cosplayers. Some cosplayers
wanted to be more than elves. They wanted to be
"other" things. This led to the word otherkin. The word
was coined in the 1990s.

Creating your role-playing character's backstory is important! It can change how you play the game.

CHAPTER 4

RELEASE YOUR INNER NERD

You, too, can be a role-playing nerd! Try one of these activities!

START WITH A SESSION ZERO!

Many session zeros happen before playing an RPG. Players meet each other. They learn the rules. They learn the setting. They create their characters.

Good role-playing needs good characters. Spend time building characters. Decide how your character looks. Decide how your character thinks. Decide how your character talks. Decide your character's strengths and flaws. Decide your character's **origin story**. Origin stories are characters' histories. They explain why characters do things. They help others better understand characters.

USE RESOURCES TO MAKE COSTUMES!

Costumes help people play their characters. They help players believe in their roles. They make characters come alive.

But costumes can be expensive. Buying them from stores costs a lot. Making them can cost a lot, too. Costumes need fabrics. Fabrics aren't cheap. Props aren't cheap, either.

There are ways to save money. Borrow items from other players. Find things in your house. Shop at thrift stores. Used things cost less.

Learn to sew. Make your own designs. **Alter** used clothes as needed. Alter means to change.

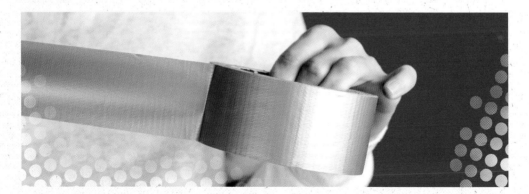

Some cosplayers use duct tape. They make costumes with tape.

Some famous people attend conventions. Actor Finn Wolfhard plays Mike in the show *Stranger Things*.

GO TO AN EVENT!

Go to a fan convention. Go to a fan meeting. Meet other fans. Search the internet. Find events near you. If there are none, host your own event. Build a community. Role-playing requires other people.

Be in character. Look like your character. Wear your costume. Talk like your character. Use body language. Stay in character. Do this the whole time. Only break your role for emergencies.

Being out of character means being yourself. Players and characters are different. Players can be more than one character. That's why role-playing is fun!

TIP #1

BE CURIOUS. ASK QUESTIONS. GOOD ROLE-PLAYERS BELIEVE IN THEIR CHARACTERS. THEY'RE GOOD ACTORS. THEY DON'T CARE WHAT OTHERS THINK. THEY'RE NOT AFRAID OF LOOKING SILLY. PLAY ALONG. GO WITH THE FLOW.

TIP #2

ROLE-PLAYERS WANT TO HAVE FUN. PLAYING EVIL CHARACTERS IS NOT AN EXCUSE FOR BAD BEHAVIOR. DON'T BULLY. BE KIND. BE RESPECTFUL. FOCUS ON HAVING FUN.

TIP #3

NOT EVERYONE IS INTO ROLE-PLAYING. MAKE SURE OTHERS KNOW YOU'RE IN CHARACTER. ASK FOR CONSENT WHEN ACTING IN CHARACTER. CONSENT MEANS PERMISSION.

TIP #4

PEOPLE MIGHT WANT TO TAKE PICTURES. THEY NEED YOUR CONSENT.

TIP #5

ROLE-PLAYING IS INCLUSIVE. IT IS OPEN TO EVERYONE. PLAYERS CAN TAKE ON ANY ROLES. THEY CAN BE MEN. THEY CAN BE WOMEN. THEY CAN BE DIFFERENT TYPES OF PEOPLE. KNOW YOUR CHARACTERS. RESPECT THEIR BACKGROUNDS.

TIP #6

CHARACTERS GROW. THEY LEARN THINGS OVER TIME. FEEL FREE TO MAKE CHANGES. DON'T GET STUCK.

TIP #7

SOME COSPLAYERS WEAR COSTUMES FOR HOURS. THIS CAN GET TIRING. IT CAN ALSO GET HOT. AIM FOR COMFORT.

GLOSSARY

alter (AWL-ter) to change or make little changes as needed

ancient (AYN-shuhnt) from a time long ago

buffs (BUFS) fans who know a lot about a specific topic

campaign (kam-PAYN) a series of games with the same players, characters, and settings

conventions (kuhn-VEN-shuhnz) large meetings of fans who come together to talk about and learn more about a shared interest

cosplay (KAHZ-play) the practice of dressing up as a character from a movie, book, or video game

English Renaissance (NG-lish RE-nuh-sahns) an era of cultural revival in England during the 1400s, 1500s, and 1600s

expos (EK-spohz) large public exhibitions

fandoms (FAN-duhmz) communies of fans; combines "fanatic" and "kingdom"

game masters (GAYM MA-sterz) people who organize and oversee a role-playing game by narrating the story and deciding the rules; shortened to GMs

origin story (OR-uh-juhn STOR-ee) the background or history of a character

original characters (uh-RIH-juh-nuhl KER-ik-terz) characters that are created by players; shortened to OCs

player characters (PLAY-er KER-ik-terz) fictional characters played by players

premade characters (PREE-mayd KER-ik-terz) characters that already exist in a role-playing game

quests (KWESTS) adventures or journeys

reenactments (ree-uh-NAK-muhntz) events where people act out historical events

role (ROHL) a character

role-playing (ROHL-play-ing) the act of pretending to be another character; shortened to RP

role-playing games (ROHL-play-ing GAYMZ) games in which players take on the personas of characters; shortened to RPGs

war games (WOHR GAYMZ) strategy games in which 2 or more players command opposing forces in a battle

LEARN MORE

Han, Yaya, Allison DeBlasio, and Joey Marsocci. *1,000 Incredible Costume and Cosplay Ideas: A Showcase of Creative Characters from Anime, Manga, Video Games, Movies, Comics, and More.* London: Quarry Books, 2013.

Hicks, Gabriel. *A Kid's Guide to Tabletop RPGs: Exploring Dice, Game Systems, Role-playing, and More!* New York: Running Press Kids, 2021.

Ratcliffe, Amy. *A Kid's Guide to Fandom Exploring Fan-Fic, Cosplay, Gaming, Podcasting, and More in the Geek World!* New York: Running Press Kids, 2021.

INDEX

NERDS RULE!

THE WONDERFUL WORLD OF NERDOM IS FULL OF COLOR AND FUN. AS DETAILS ABOUT POPULAR TOPICS IN THE NERD COMMUNITY ARE REVEALED, READERS OF THIS HI-LO SERIES WILL ADMIRE THE CREATIVITY, COMMUNITY, AND PASSION ONLY NERDS BRING TO THE TABLE.

BOOKS IN THIS SERIES:

Nerding Out About DIY

Nerding Out About Fantasy

Nerding Out About Gaming

Nerding Out About Japanese Popular Culture

Nerding Out About Role-Playing

Nerding Out About Science Fiction

45th Parallel Press Titles Feature:
High interest topics with accessible reading levels
Considerate vocabulary
Engaging content and fascinating facts
Clear text and formatting
Compelling photos

ISBN-13: 978-1668939369

9 781668 939369

45TH PARALLEL PRESS